Main Street-Colorado.com

Business Training Series

❦

WHY YOU SHOULD LEARN TO MANUFACTURE YOUR OWN PRODUCTS!

❦

Professional Instruction By

Timothy M. Braun
&
Anita M. Braun

© 2018 Timothy M. Braun & Anita M. Braun

www.MainStreet-Colorado.com

Sangre de Cristo Publishing, Inc.
Cripple Creek, Colorado

Printed in the United States of America.

Cover design by Timothy M. Braun

Published by Sangre de Cristo Publishing, Inc.,

P.O. Box 1003,

Cripple Creek, CO. 80813

Kindle digital edition available at www.amazon.com

WELCOME TO THE WONDERFUL WORLD OF MANUFACTURING!

Don't be nervous about the word "manufacture"; it is synonymous with the word "make", as in 'make your own products'.

Definition of Manufacturing from WEBSTER:

1: something made from raw materials by hand or by machinery

2: the process of making wares by hand or by machinery especially when carried on systematically with division of labor

3: the act or process of producing something

Mid 16th century (denoting something made by hand): from French (re-formed by association with Latin

manu factum 'made by hand'), from Italian manifattura.

Manufacturing your own products is very easy and much more profitable than buying/selling products from a Multi Level Marketing company or from a wholesaler!

Are you really making any $$ with Avon, Mary Kay, Amway, Tupperware, Legal Shield, Young Living, DoTerra or any other MLM (Multi Level Marketing)? Are you working hard, making sales, but don't seem to see many profits because of all the fees and hidden costs associated with your business? It has been shown that up to 99% of those selling in an MLM don't really make any REAL $$.

Who is really making all the money? It's the manufacturers, the people at the top.

Do you have a retail business and would like to add custom-made manufactured products to your line that your customers would love? Would you like a GREAT home business manufacturing your own products that are needed and customers love?

Would you like to be at the top? Would you like to make $$ and REALLY control your own destiny?

Learn how to manufacture your own line of T-Shirts, Bath & Body & Home products, and a whole line of sublimation products!! You can literally have fun; even make it a family business, and possibly turn your products into a multi-million dollar business! There are no quotas or goals to meet. Work and learn at your own pace. There are no sales meetings you have to attend, no sales tiers to work towards. Your rewards are the goals you set and reach for yourself. You are your own boss.

We started manufacturing our own products over six years ago and have learned much in the different industries, while selling hundreds of thousand of dollars in products. It was hard starting out, as we had to purchase large quantities of everything to get decent pricing in the Bath & Body & Home business in order to make a good profit. We had to purchase thousands of dollars of bottles and pumps and caps and fragrances and lotion bases. It was extremely expensive, but there was nowhere we could get just what we wanted starting out with decent pricing. We had over $10,000 invested just in fragrances and essential oils. This is one of the areas we help you out getting started. We pass along much of our savings that we have by purchasing in large volumes to you, no matter how much you purchase, because we want you to succeed. Want 2 or 3 of a certain color of bottles or caps? No problem. We are here to help you along your path to success.

In the T-shirt and sublimation business, there are ways to save money, and we will teach you those also.

Most of the items we will be teaching you to manufacture, we have sold thousands of them, all manufactured by us. We do know what we are talking about.

Whether you are a stay-at-home mom or dad, retired, handicapped or whatever, you can create a business that makes real $$ -- right from your home!
When you manufacture/make your own products you can make upwards of 80%+ profits on your products, or upwards of 600-800% ROI (Return on investment) by starting your own line of products.
They are ultra easy to produce and we show you everything, step by step!

Why sell someone else's products when you can sell your own? You can wholesale or retail for the greater profit. Advertise your products as ***Made In America!*** Most national brands can't say or do that as most are manufactured overseas. Plus, many customers will pay a premium for ***Made in America***.

Build your business by selling to school or non-profit fundraisers; sell on Etsy, at fairs, craft shows, churches, your own website, social media, etc. Your world is unlimited to where you can sell retail, or wholesale your products to local businesses. The sky is the limit.

If you never take that first step, nothing ever happens. Every time you resist something new, you hinder yourself from achieving anything. Fear actually stops you from going forward. This is an opportunity, a chance to take an opportunity, to connect with someone who has done it and use their experience to take yourself to the next level. Wherever you are today, just start! Take charge of your future!!

1. Do I need any prior knowledge to get started?
A. No, we teach you everything, from the very basics to the technical.

2. Is there a membership or initiation fee?
A: No, the only costs are the supplies you select to start to manufacture your products.
All businesses have expenses associated with them. You will need to purchase the e-book on the business that interests you and any supplies in order to manufacture the products.

3. What supplies will I need?

A: We suggest you start manufacturing just a few products, get used to the process and then add products as you feel comfortable, obtain orders or want to add to your line.

4. Where do I learn how to manufacture and obtain training?

A. We have videos planned for the future, so until we have our videos finished, you will be able to simply follow the instructions for each item you manufacture from our e-books. We will provide all the documentation you need for you to refer to.

5. Do I need a business or a sales tax license?

A. In order for us to not charge sales tax (where we have to) you will need a business license if your city/county/state requires one to do business. You will also need a sales tax license if your city/county/state requires one. In Colorado, you will probably need both. Although you won't charge sales tax on wholesale sales, all sales will usually still have to be reported if you are a business.

Q. Can I get started without a business license or sales tax certificate?

A. Yes, you can order your supplies to get started, but we may have to charge sales tax in Colorado. You are always better off with a business license.

7. What other Bath & Body & Home products do you supply and teach?

A. Are you ready? Face Creams, Face Masks, Body Mists, Body Sprays, Foaming Hand Soaps, Shaving Butters, Perfumes (Oil Based and Alcohol Based), Foot Balms, Moisturizing Lotion Bars, Nail & Cuticle Conditioner, Ultimate Body & Skin Therapy, Hand Balm, Lip Balms, Room & Linen Sprays, All-natural base Glycerin Shea Butter Bar Soaps, All-natural base Glycerin Cocoa Butter Bar Soaps, All-natural base Glycerin Goat Milk Bar Soaps, All-natural base Glycerin Aloe Vera Bar Soaps, Bath Bombs, Fragranced Bath Salts, Body Wash, Fragranced Body Salt Scrubs, Shampoo & Conditioner, Men's Aftershave Gel, Beard Oil, Men's Moisturizer, Men's Body Wash, Men's Body Spray, Men's Spray Cologne, Men's Hand & Body Lotion, Men's Shaving Butter, Candles, Massage Candles… and more!

Contact us for more information while we populate our website with e-books, instructions and more questions and answers. You will need to be approved to access the manufacturing part of the website (www.MainStreet-Colorado.com) that has the deeply discounted pricing, instructions and videos.

Interested? **Get started now!!** 719-689-3330. We are open from 10 a.m.-5 p.m. Rocky Mountain time zone or email us anytime at **MainStreetColorado@gmail.com**. You can also visit us at The Hitchin' Post, 333 E. Bennett Ave., in Cripple Creek, CO.

Let Me Repeat Myself!

If you never take the first step, nothing ever happens. Every time you resist something new, you hinder yourself from achieving anything. Fear actually stops you from going forward. This is an opportunity, a chance to take an opportunity, to connect with someone who has done it and use their experience to take yourself to the next level. Wherever you are today, just start! Take charge of your future!!

Bath & Body & Home Products Business

Starting your own business in the Bath & Body & Home industry is a great way to add income to your household. You can build your business in your spare time, you can learn as you go and you will meet many new people. Most Bath & Body &

Home lines are are multi-national, large corporate entities and are mass produced. Our niche is custom made. I can't count the number of people who ask for a specific fragrance that they can't find anywhere else, but you can also maintain the mainstream fragrances that are very popular. By also offering the essential oils and blends, you add value to your line as the large corporate types of companies producing the Bath & Body & Home lines usually won't use essential oils and they definitely won't custom make anything..

One of the things that can be a large expense that will eat into your profits is freight. Imagine having to pay freight/postage on each item you purchase from different suppliers! It just eats up your profits.

It can become very expensive! So, Instead of paying thousands of dollars on individual items like we did, you can get started with us for under $100 and make profits over 70% on your sales with no fees or hidden costs to eat up your profits! It's easy, and we'll show you how!

Starter's Path – <u>Things to Consider…</u>

As you consider whether manufacturing your own fragrance- and beauty-aids is for you, there are a few things you'd likely want to know before you risk too much.

- Who is the market you'd likely sell to?

    - Start by trying family and friends, you may be in school and maybe your classmates are part of your market. Where can you display or advertise your "goods" so people are aware they are available and the exchange (sell/purchase) can occur? Will it be by word-of-mouth? Posting flyers in your neighboring area? Mail? Website? Listed on a retailer website (e.g., Amazon, Etsy)? Or displayed on a shelf in (a) local store(s)?

- How much product should I make?

    - Start in small quantities for a few reasons:

        - You want to be able to "consistently" repeat your "recipe" in case one of them goes viral. So, document it and be precise!

        - You want to reduce risk in having to carry any fragrances/supply that doesn't move. These are supplies that end up paid for, but not selling. You certainly want to keep these to a minimum!

- You don't want a lot of cash tied up in inventory that's not moving. So, small quantities until you find the ones that sell, and then increase those supplies to increase cash flow and profits.

- How much time does it take?

  - By starting small, you also get to know how long it takes you to mix/manufacture each fragrance-/beauty-aid. The time to manufacturer each product multiplied by the daily or weekly demand for the product tells you how much time it will require from you to manufacture the products that are selling.

- How many supplies should I buy?

  - Start with small quantities to reduce invested cash and mitigate risks.

- As your demand increases, increase your supplies appropriately. There is usually a savings the larger the quantities of supplies purchased, but too many supplies put you at risk.

- Balance risk and profit. A lot of supplies on-hand adds cash invested in inventory that has yet to see a demand. However, the larger the quantity of supplies you order, the lower the cost of those supplies. You basically have two costs in your products; (a) the supplies to manufacture the products, and (b) your time to change the supplies into a product.

- A little help with how to figure your "costs," "paycheck" and "profit."

   Product you have invested time in manufacturing, but have not sold, is also value you may never get back if it doesn't sell. So, starting small keeps your time vested in non-moving inventory to a minimum, and focused on those products that are selling.

   After paying for all your supplies, profits may remain and can be used to expand your inventory, expand your paycheck and profits in the future. Of course, whether your paycheck takes all the profits is a business decision. You can decide if you are able and want to expand your market and sales, and continue down this path to larger sales, paychecks and profits.

We can help. We teach you how to manufacture your products, develop your labeling, provide you with the supplies in small enough quantities to reduce your invested cash and lower risk. We hope this will help alleviate as much stress to starting your own business and using your profits to help pay for a vacation, a trip, gifts, or maybe even upgrade your mode of transportation or quality of living space. Of course, we hope it simply helps you enjoy a higher quality of life – whatever that may mean to you and your loved ones.

One of the first things you want to consider is where you want to position yourself in the industry. What do I mean by positioning yourself? It means at what level of sophistication do you want to see your products. Do you want to be on the level of a cheap discount, generic, bulk type product or one of the more sophisticated products that cost more? Do you want to sell your 8 oz lotion for $9.99, $16.99, $19.99 or $25.99? What type of customer are you selling to and whom do you want to attract? In addition, if you start your products out at, say, at $19.99, it leaves you room to have a special or a sale price, which is lower, but still makes a nice profit.

There are literally hundreds of cheap knock-off brands and you will get lost in the crowd if that is your customer. Position yourself as a higher-end product and you will attract that type of customer for even more of your products. If they believe they are getting value for their money, they will continue to purchase

Let's talk about labels for a moment. This is probably what is going to attract your customer more than anything else. It's basic marketing. If you make a quality label that attracts the eye, you will be more successful than using a plain label that doesn't attract anything. A quality label also will help you position your products at a higher level. So spend the time necessary to develop a quality label. I can help you by giving you the information as to where these designs and logos can be done very inexpensively ($5-$20).

You will need labels for each item, usually in at least three sizes (2oz, 4oz, 8oz). We will show you what printers to use or print them for you if you wish, or supply the sheets of labels for you to print your own. Your labels are an important part of your

16

products. Take time to design a great label. No one will be attracted to a product with a drab or dull label. It has to make your products stand out.

I always suggest using a gloss or a weatherproof label. It makes the colors you use brighter, makes them "pop". It also holds up better in a bathroom environment where many products will be used.

You may ask, 'how do you do that?" One of the easiest ways is to get the right printer when you start out or when you've made enough money. I'll also show you the best place to get your printer. Now, you can have the labels printed by a commercial printer, but starting out, that can get very expensive. With just lotions, if you offer three different lotions with three different sizes, that's nine different labels you will have to have printed and most of time, at a minimum, you'll have to have hundreds of each printed.

I suggest to all just starting out, invest in an Epson color printer. Why Epson? There are two different types of ink used in printers, dye and pigment. Epson is the only printer that uses a pigment ink. This is what you want as the ink sits on top of the label/paper, makes the image "pop", not into the label/paper as a dye ink does. Also, the ink is "archival," it's supposed to last almost a hundred years without fading, etc. In addition, I will show you how and where to purchase your ink so it costs you practically NOTHING! You know those $10, $15, $20 ink cartridges? Never again!!

Some will ask, why not a color laser printer? Well, I have tried and sampled many color laser printers. I don't like them because you really can't get a true red out of them, and a good color red attracts the eye. They all seemed very dull or had an orange tint to them. Maybe if you purchased an $1000- $2000 printer, you might get the quality you need, but I tried many of the office versions that were in the $200-$500 range and they didn't live up to my expectations.

To help you out, I'll even print your labels for you, but you have to obtain your designs first. I'll give you the sizes your designs need to be for me to print the labels you choose. I charge an extra $2.00/ page for printing plus a one-time layout fee.

Q. ---I'd like to see an example of making over 70% profit on my first order under $75 of Bath & Body & Home products! (Total Cost: $71.18; Total sales from those costs: $254.85; Total profit from those sales: $183.74)

A. All right, here goes: A gallon of our finest lotion will cost you $48.95. That will make (16) - 8oz lotions; 15 will cost:

((128 oz) / 16) x 15 = $45.89). 3 bottles of different fragrances will be $2.90 each or $8.70. Usage will be 83% of the 3 bottles or $7.22 for 15 - 8 oz lotions. 15 clear pumps will be 58.5¢ ea or $8.78. (15) 8 oz Boston bottles will be 49.6¢ ea or $7.29. A sheet of 15 glossy labels is $2.00. Add them all up and it comes to $71.18.

You shouldn't sell this 8 oz lotion for less than $16.99 (you can sell it for whatever you want). $71.18 total cost divided by (15) - 8oz lotions, comes to your cost of $4.745/ea or $12.245 profit ea. $4.745 divided by the selling price of $16.99 equals your cost of 27.9% of the selling price or 72.1% profit. All of this is at the start-up discount. As you grow and order more quantities, your discount becomes greater and thus your profit becomes greater.

Let's look at the 4 oz lotions. A gallon of our finest lotion, again, will cost you $48.95. If we were to make (15)-4 oz lotions that is 46.8% of the gallon. That cost would be $22.91. 2 bottles of different fragrances will be $2.90 each or $5.80, and that will give you 30 ml of fragrance. We will only need 18.75 ml at the most, which is 62.5% of $5.80 or $3.63. 15 metal dispensing caps will be 63¢ ea or $9.45. (15) 4 oz Boston bottles will be 46¢ ea or $6.90. A sheet of 15 glossy labels is

$2.00. Add them all up and it comes to $44.89. Your cost is $2.992 / bottle.

I sell these 4 oz lotions for 9.99 (you can sell it for whatever you want). Your cost is 29.9% of sales & gives you a 70.1% profit margin.

Q. ---I'd like to see another example of a different item making over 70% on my first order under $100!

A. All right, here goes: A gallon of our Premium body butter will cost you $46.95. That will make (16) - 8oz body butters; 15 will cost ((128 oz) / 16) x 15 = $44.015). 3 bottles of different fragrances will be $2.90 each or $8.70. Usage will be 83.3% of the 3 bottles or $7.25 for 15 - 8 oz body butters. (15) 8 oz Double Wall jars will be $1.30 ea or $19.50. A sheet of 15 glossy labels is $2.00. Add them all up and it comes to $72.76.

You shouldn't sell this 8 oz body butter for less than $16.99 (but you can sell it for whatever you want). $72.76 total cost divided by (15) - 8oz body butter comes to your cost of $4.85/ea or $12.14 profit ea. $4.85 divided by the selling price of $16.99 equals your cost of 28.5% of the selling price or 71.5% profit. All of this is at the start-up discount. As you grow and order more quantities, your discount becomes greater and thus your profit becomes greater.

Q. Have another?

A. **Want an 80% profit margin?** Let's do roll-on perfume. This is one of our better profit items and they sell very well. A glass bottle with roller and cap will cost you $1.49/ea. 15 of them will be 22.35. A bottle of 4 oz body oil will be $5.99 and that will give you enough for 15 roll-ons. You use 2 ml of fragrance or essential oil in each roll-on. 2 bottles of different fragrances will be $2.90 each or $5.80, and that will give you fragrance for 15 roll-ons. A sheet of glossy labels is $2.00. Add them all up and it comes to $36.14.

I sell this 10 ml roll-on perfume for $12.99 (you can sell it for whatever you want). $39.07 total cost divided by (15) - 10 ml roll-on perfumes comes to your cost of $2.41/ea or $10.58 profit ea. $2.41 divided by the selling price of $12.99 equals your cost of 18.5% of the selling price or 81.5% profit. All of this is at the start-up discount. If you add the velour perfume bag & plastic bag/label, there will be a small additional cost. As you grow and order more quantities, your discount becomes greater and thus your profit becomes greater.

Q. What other products do you have?

We have all the products we named before and more.

As an added benefit for you, we also have our line of essential oils and fragrances you can sell for a nice profit. This is one of our best selling items and you can make up to 60% profit on each sale! We have over 220 different essential and fragrance oils.

We also have Muscle Freeze, massage oils, many different body oils and other items you may want to sell, all with great profit margins.

The following is a spreadsheet of the examples we just told you about including a couple other items.

	Bottle	Jar	Cost Base	Label	Cap	Pump	Frag	ml-frag	Sugg Sell @	Cost	Profit	profit %
Masage Oil-$29.95/Gal												
Masage Oil-8 oz	$0.49		$1.871	$0.133	$0.63				$12.99	$3.12	$9.87	75.95%
Masage Oil-4 oz	$0.46		$0.935	$0.133	$0.63				$8.99	$2.16	$6.83	76.00%
Masage Oil-2 oz	$0.41		$0.467	$0.133	$0.63				$5.99	$1.64	$4.35	72.62%
Lotion-GMHS-$48.95/Gal												
8 oz	$0.49		$3.059	$0.133		$0.585	$0.465	2.500	$16.99	$4.73	$12.26	72.15%
4 oz	$0.46		$1.529	$0.133	$0.630		$0.232	1.250	$9.99	$2.98	$7.01	70.13%
2 oz	$0.41		$0.764	$0.133	$0.630		$0.116	0.625	$6.99	$2.05	$4.94	70.63%
Lotion-Satin & Silk / Aloe & Shea - $54.95/Gal												
8 oz	$0.49		$3.434	$0.133		$0.585	$0.465	2.500	$16.99	$5.11	$11.88	69.94%
4 oz	$0.46		$1.717	$0.133	$0.630		$0.232	1.250	$9.99	$3.17	$6.82	68.25%
2 oz	$0.41		$0.858	$0.133	$0.630		$0.116	0.625	$6.99	$2.15	$4.84	69.28%
Lotion-Basic-$29.95/Gal												
8 oz	$0.49		$1.871	$0.133		$0.585	$0.465	2.500	$9.99	$3.54	$6.45	64.52%
4 oz	$0.46		$0.935	$0.133	$0.630		$0.232	1.250	$6.99	$2.39	$4.60	65.81%
2 oz	$0.41		$0.467	$0.133	$0.630		$0.116	0.625	$4.99	$1.76	$3.23	64.81%
Body Butter- Premium / Avocado Body Butter $46.95/Gal												
8 oz		$1.30	$2.928	$0.166					$16.99	$4.86	$12.13	71.40%
4 oz		$0.90	$1.464	$0.166					$9.99	$2.76	$7.23	72.35%
2 oz		$0.70	$0.732	$0.166					$6.99	$1.71	$5.28	75.48%
Roll-On Perfume												
12 ml	$1.49		$0.392	$0.133			$0.390	2.000	$12.99	$2.41	$10.59	81.49%
Shaving Butter- Men - $54.95												
8 oz		$1.27	$3.434	$0.166			$0.465	2.500	$16.99	$5.34	$11.66	68.60%
4 oz		$0.99	$1.717	$0.166			$0.232	1.250	$9.99	$3.11	$6.89	68.92%
2 oz		$0.89	$0.858	$0.166			$0.116	0.625	$6.99	$2.03	$4.96	70.96%

23

Design, Print & Sell T-Shirt Business

How To Be in Business in a Short Time for Under $900

You don't have to be a brain surgeon to start a t-shirt business. It's not easy, but it's not hard… it just takes a lot of work and a commitment to be in business for yourself. It's fun, especially when everything comes together and you start getting orders, and some will be large, large enough to pay for all your costs and you can start making a profit.

I started off very small. I just wanted to print a few shirts that I had designed for Smart Ass University, a trademark design I now use for shirts and outerwear. As the shirts gained popularity, I branched out into other areas such as hats, tote bags, tea towels, aprons, etc. I let everyone know I could do shirts for them overnight, and that was the key. Everyone wanted shirts NOW! Screen printers can't do that; no one else around could. You'd be surprised at how many people wait until the last minute to order shirts.

A few years ago, I approached two local stores that agreed to carry some of my shirts. They started out with about 6 different designs. In one summer season, they sold approximately 2500 shirts. They kept adding more designs and even asked me to design and print some shirts they wanted to try. That's where you have a leg up on every screen printer. You can design and print a couple of FULL COLOR shirts for anyone for a couple of dollars, basically the cost of the shirts.

A screen printer will charge well over a hundred dollars for a two or three-color design, just for a couple of shirts. That's because they have a large process to go through. It's costly and labor intensive.

You can sit down at a computer, print out a transfer in a couple minutes, press it in a couple more minutes and you're done, with less than a dollar in costs plus the cost of the shirt. Who do you think a customer will go with to try a new design??

I now print thousands of shirts every year, and I have perfected the process, which I will share with you. I will take you through a process to begin printing shirts that covers most of the experience I have gained and most of the mistakes I have made. There's no need to make the same mistakes, and believe me, there were a lot of them. Some of them were very expensive and were doozies!!

There are a few things you will need to get started, namely a heat press, an Epson printer, special inks, special transfer paper, Teflon sheets and pillows, and of course, shirts.

Buy an expensive heat press or an inexpensive one? We will discuss that.

An Epson printer is needed for the same reasons as stated in the Bath & Body section, but even more so as you need the option it has for laying down heavier ink than usual and you will need the pigmented ink. I show you where to get your special inks and paper and all the other necessary items to perfect your business.

How much can you make on the average T-Shirt?

Right now, light colored shirts (white, light grey, light pink, light blue, natural (light brown)), small to extra-large right now are going for about $1.86 each. The dark colored shirts are a few cents more. The average use of transfer paper I teach you about, and how to save more, for each shirt would be about $.45 each. The ink, if you purchase at the place I teach you, will be about $.02 each. (If you skip or miss that part and only purchase the Epson cartridges, it will be a lot more! **A lot more!!**) So, your total cost will be about $2.33 per shirt. I sell these shirts all day long for $14.99. My profit per shirt is $12.71. I wholesale them for 50% of that in quantity, so I make $5.17 each (Usually the order has to be at least 20 shirts. Many of them are over 100). I can whip out 100 shirts in 2-3 hours. Not a bad profit.

I sell the 2x-3x sizes for $2—3.00 more and the 4x-5x sizes for $4-6.00 more.

One of the great things I will teach you is where to get plastisol, one-color transfers up to 9" x 12" for $.15 each. Yes, 15 cents each! I also teach you where to get full-color plastisol 9" x 12" transfers for $1.15 each. I use these for shirts that I sell a lot of and I explain to you why. Plastisol is the material used to screen print shirts and it is also used for our transfers.

There are also legal issues with infant or children's shirts I explain to you and tell you where to go to get registered. A law was passed called the Consumer Product Safety Improvement Act of 2008, that requires all kinds of testing on children's (up to age 12) wear. There are big fines for not following it. You can get a waiver from the federal government if you sell less than 1 million dollars a year and I think all of us qualify for that, but all the shirts have to have special labeling.

Don't know where to go to get your designs done cheaply? I tell you where you can get great designs done for a little as $5.00! I have used them several times and they have always done a great job for me!

You can get all this information and more in our e-book for instant download, or in a printed book, "Design, Print & Sell T-Shirts" available on Etsy, Amazon or our website, MainStreet-Colorado.com.

LEARN SUBLIMATION

Sublimation is the transition of a substance directly from the solid phase to the gas phase without passing through an intermediate liquid phase. (Wikipedia)

As I am writing this, I am in the middle of sublimating 100 mugs.

When sublimation inks are heated to 400°F, they turn into a gas and permanently bond to 100% polyester fabric or items that have a polymer coating. The image is transferred **INTO** the surface and **not ONTO** the surface. The result is a premium, full-color, photographic-quality image that will not crack, peel or wash away from the substrate to which it was applied.

You may not know it, but if you have a heat press, you have the ability to substantially increase your sales to your present customers with other great promotional items. T-Shirts are a great source of revenue and a great customer base builder, but why just stop at shirts and sweatshirts? Most customers, especially retail customers you wholesale to, always want more merchandise that will sell. You can supply them! Just ask them!

What about schools and non-profit groups that constantly sell promotional items to raise funds? Do you think they only want to sell candy, popcorn and cookies? The answer is a great big **"NO"**. They want saleable items, just like retailers, that will sell and make them money. That is the name of the game, making money, whether it's for you or for the groups you sell to.

The question becomes 'what do I make to increase my sales?' So far, I've chosen about ten different items, which, for me sell very well. The items I use my heat press with are the following:

Mousepads & Coasters—How many people and businesses use mousepads? How many businesses use mousepads as promotional give-a-ways? Lots. Making mousepads and coasters are probably the easiest of all the sublimations. You can obtain coasters in foam rubber or hardboard.

Custom Clocks- Your customer will want to put photos on the face of the clocks and businesses will put their logos on them.

Ornaments (Christmas, etc.) A great profit maker! Businesses will put their logos on Christmas ornaments and small cities and towns will put their emblems on them with the year to celebrate Christmas every year.

Magnets & Signs: Custom signs & magnets can be a real money-maker. The hardboard signs have a high gloss finish and really look nice. When your customers see your samples, they tend to be an easy selling item. You can purchase many different sizes of signs. I use mostly white gloss hardboard tiles as they give great results and the colors are vivid. You can drill small holes in the corners and string a wire hanger or use double stick tape to hang them. Aluminum signs are also available in many sizes. Many businesses use magnets and they are available in hardboard or aluminum in several sizes.

Ceramic & Glass Tiles: Ceramic and glass tiles can be a beautiful addition to any room. You can frame them, use them as magnets, as a mural, or use them individually. You can create stunning works of art. Tile murals are huge profit makers!

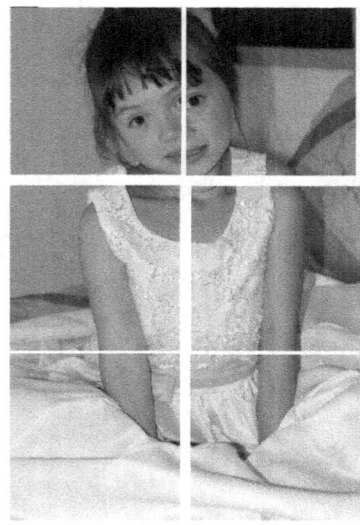
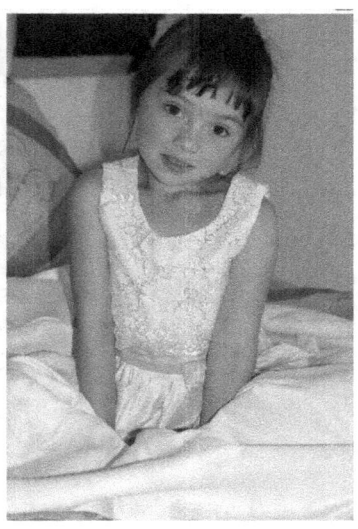

License Plates & License Plate Frames – Again, businesses (auto dealers) will put their name and place on the frames. I've found that schools and businesses will also put their names and logos on the license plates.

The actual process of sublimation is very simple. If you can print a shirt with a heat transfer, you can sublimate any of the above items. Some other items are a little more complicated, but most of your money will probably be made with some of these items. About the only difference between heat transfers and sublimation is the temperature of the process.

Mugs-THE <u>REAL</u> MONEY MAKER! If you invest in sublimation, you will definitely want to purchase a mug press or two. This is perhaps the best investment as EVERYONE uses coffee mugs and I have literally sold thousands of them. I don't care who they are; businesses, schools, non-profits, individuals.

etc., everyone uses them for promotions and their own use. A mug press will also print water bottles.

A few of the mugs we make

Put "Mug Press" into a Google search and you'll get anything from $49.95 to $289.00; there is no need to buy expensive mug presses that some places will try to sell you. Some of the less expensive ones work just fine.

What is sublimation going to cost?

1.) **Printer**--First, you will need another printer, as you will be using special ink we'll talk about in a few minutes. **Refillable cartridges**— I show you where to get your special inks and refillable ink cartridges to keep your costs low.

2.) **Paper**- You have to use a special paper for sublimation printing. It's not expensive and I'll list a few places for you to purchase it.

3.) **Sublimation Ink**-- There is one company that sells their sublimation ink for the small format printers we use, and they are very expensive, about $259-$400 for four 125ml bottles. However, I will show you several companies that are selling sublimation ink for a very reasonable price, about 10-15% of the above price.

4.) **High-heat tape**-- It is used to tape the images to your mugs, signs, etc. This is a must as you don't want the images on your paper moving at any time. I'll show you where to get it.

5.) **Spray adhesive**-- Some companies sell a special adhesive for this purpose, but I'll show you what you can get from Walmart that is just as good

The above items will take care of most sublimation. There are a few other specialty items you will need if you get into plates, shot glasses or things like that, that we will discuss.

Printing Out Your Mug Designs--

Printing out your images is a very important step, and if you do it right, you wont have to measure anything to get your images placed right on your mugs and they will go on straight. I will teach you and show you the patterns to use. You will have a pattern you can use for all your different images, saving you tons of time and lost mugs. You will ruin many mugs (like I did at the beginning as I didn't have an instructor) if you don't closely follow these steps. I've done a lot of work for you here that you won't have to duplicate later and lose a lot of mugs in the process.

Don't know where to go to get your designs done cheaply? I tell you where you can get great designs done for a little as $5.00! I have used them many times and they have always done a great job for me!

You can get all this information and more in our e-book for instant download, or in a print copy, "Learn Sublimation For Great Profits!" available on Etsy, Amazon or our website, MainStreet-Colorado.com.

God Bless and we wish you great profits!!
Tim & Anita Braun

Interested? Get started now! Email us your name, address & phone # to MainStreetColorado@gmail.com, with the requested information and we'll send you your password to access the manufacturing section of MainStreet-Colorado.com to make all your purchases and get started on your new business!

Notes & Disclaimers:

- All pricing is subject to change.

- Sangre de Cristo Publishing, Inc is not responsible for the products you create from our supplies, recipes, or instructions. You alone are responsible for product and recipe testing to ensure compatibility and safety.

- Overpours or underpours may affect the percentages of profits in statements above.